Traffic

A BOOK OF OPPOSITES

by Betsy and Giulio Maestro

Crown Publishers, Inc. New York

The text of this book is set in 30 point Melior
The illustrations were prepared by the artist
with halftone overlays, for blue, red and yellow

Library of Congress Cataloging in Publication Data
Maestro, Betsy.
Traffic.
SUMMARY: Text and illustrations introduce words with
opposite meanings such as over and under, big and little, and front and back.
1. English language—Synonyms and antonyms—Juvenile literature.
[1. English language—Synonyms and antonyms]
I. Maestro, Giulio. II. Title.
PE1591.M33   1981   428.1   80-29641
ISBN 0-517-54427-X

Traffic

A BOOK OF OPPOSITES

Go home, little car.
Go **over** the bridge.

Go **under** the bridge.

Take a **left** turn.

Take a **right** turn.

Stop at the red light.

Creep in **slow** traffic.

Move **fast** on the highway.

Pass a **big** car.

Pass a **little** car.

Here is an **empty** truck.

There is a **full** truck.

The tollgate is **closed.**

The tollgate is **open.**

Drive on a **narrow** road.

Drive on a **wide** road.

Go through a **dark** tunnel.

Come out into the **light.**

There goes a **long** train.

Here comes a **short** one.

That house is **far** away.

This house is **near.**

Climb the **high** hill.

Go down to the **low** valley.

This is the **front** of a bus.

Here is the **back** of the bus.

Drive through the **day**.

Drive through the **night**.

You are home, little car.
Good night!